THE SORCERESS CAGLIASTRO

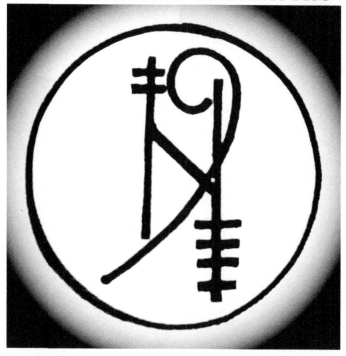

THE IRON RING

25 SIGILS
DARK CIRCLES
SIGILS FROM THE IRON RING

THE SORCERESS CAGLIASTRO
BLOOD SORCERESS, NECROMANCER IN THE HANDS OF 9

COPYRIGHT 2014

25 SIGILS

The first book in the on going offering of
DARK CIRCLES by
THE SORCERESS CAGLIASTRO
Blood Sorceress, Necromancer in the
hands of 9

All of the Sigils herein are Iron Ring originals. They have all been tested and utilized by
THE SORCERESS CAGLIASTRO
Blood Sorceress, Necromancer in the hands of 9 – in partnership with others willing to test the materials and gather data.

MY BOOKS....

I write in large print because as I have previously stated, most of my readers are not fond of bright lights, and are known to write notes in the books they use most frequently...

This book is a list of Sigils and the operations needed to enact them. All of the sigils in this book have been well tested and are Iron Ring Originals.

This is NOT a novel. It is not a highly edited master grimoire, it is not an art project. It is a practical manual meant for use in the most practical way. If you are concerned with syntax then you may consider putting down this extremely valuable tool and waiting for my next novel so that you can dissect that...however for now, on this date – herein is my offering....

I created these sigils over decades of work... They are, for the most part, Iron Ring Originals. They are protected by copyright. This means that those of you who have a penchant to share my writings on scrib and other thieving sites consider that this is the fourteenth book I have written on the subject so no cloak will hide you - as I have seen it all....

I point this out because I want to step – NOT SO DELICATELY - on the subject of the pirating of my work. If you do it – I will enact Sorcery upon you. Clarity keeps people safe - and now that has been said.....

There will be at very least two other books containing sigils following the publication of this one. I chose these 25 because they are of a similar 'weight'. By this I mean that they require similar commitment and participation. They are not of a similar subject – only a similar density.

HOW TO USE THIS BOOK

This book is formatted as follows…
The Sigils are **first** presented only with a title, thereby offering a brief description. I suggest the reader spend time observing the sigils first in that simple format.

OBSERVATION YIELDS THOUGHT.

I chose to write these Sigil books in a particular format that would offer an opportunity for use by novices to the work, as well as an additional category noted as SKILLED STUDENTS.   I included this section to serve the individuals who have studied with me over time.

This section includes information regarding the 4 Pillars.

The 4 Pillars of the Science of Sorcery are The Boxes, Directional Sorcery, The Static Practice/Chaos Void and the Iron Ring. One can become introduced to them through the **Blood Sorcery Bible Volume II – Striking The Target**. This is the most important one of my books on the subject.

That being said, the SKILLED STUDENT section is for those individuals who have studied through classes and individual instructions with me and have a working knowledge of the 4 Pillars.

Next, after the observation of the sigil, go to SECTION II, INITIAL IMPRESSIONS. **Take a moment to write your initial impression of the Sigil in this notes section AS THIS IS VITAL. Doing so will provide a baseline for future troubleshooting.**

When you are ready to use a sigil proceed to **SECTION III-UTILIZATION**. Here you will find directives regarding how to create and use each Sigil. Continue to use the **notes** section to record information regarding your process and outcome as **data is vital in the Science of Sorcery**.

SECTION III – UTILIZATION is broken down into the following categories:

OVERVIEW – basic intended usage

DECONSTRUCTION – a light review regarding the specific symbols in the sigil

EXECUTION – how best to create the sigil

BLOOD APPLICATION – where appropriate

RITUAL – details about the ritual and/or practical applications of usage

SKILLED STUDENTS – This section is provided for and directed at my students as previously stated, who have a grasp of the 4 PILLARS of the Science of Sorcery which are The Boxes, Directional Sorcery, The Static Practice/Chaos Void and the Iron Ring. There are a few Master Student notations...you know who you are...

Blood Sorcery of course is the foundation and the most vital component of the work in which students develop expertise. The 4 Pillars are used with Blood Sorcery to offer the best outcome. To study these materials visit

www.cagliastrotheironring.com, go to the Wednesday Night Core Classes section and obtain a 4 week package. The classes are on-going.

Also note that questions can be sent to me via the **CONTACT and STUDY** information at the end of this book.

Additionally a set of cards containing this group of 25 Sigils will be available before the end of 2014. To order the deck send an email requesting an update on availability to the following email address....

sorceresscagliastro@gmail.com

TABLE OF SIGILS

I - To release yourself from the traps of kindness, social mores, and foregiveness

II - To Remain Focused

III - To Re-Set

IV - To separate one from potential property

V - To Uncover Truth

VI - To understand Sorcery

VII - Unlock Further Research that may be restricted

VIII - To use sex in a persuasive way

IX - Enact vengance annonymously

X - Weight Loss

XI - To Be Able to Tell the Difference between Facts and Lies

XII - "Fearless" revelation of the self

XIII - To Become Unemotional In Any Circumstance

XIV - To Cause Chaos in Another's Sorcery/Magic

XV - To Cause One to "Drown" In Their Own Lies

XVI - To Deplete An Energy or Adversary or the energy of an enemy

XVII - To Encourage Dark Energy

XVIII -To Increase One's Ability to Develop Ritual

25S – I

TO RELEASE YOURSELF FROM TRAPS OF KINDNESS, SOCIAL MORES AND FOREGIVENESS REFLEXES

25S – II

TO REMAIN FOCUSED

25S – III
TO RE-SET THE SELF OR THE SITUATION

25S – IV
TO SEPARATE ONE FROM POTENTIAL PROPERTY

25S – V

TO UNCOVER TRUTH

25S – VI

TO UNDERSTAND SORCERY

25S – VII

UNLOCK FURTHER RESEARCH THAT MAY
BE RESTRICTED

25S –VIII

TO USE SEX IN A PERSUASIVE WAY

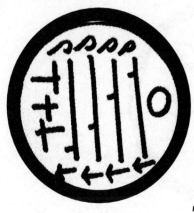

25S – IX

TO ENACT VENGANCE ANNONYMOUSLY

25S – X

WEIGHT LOSS

25S – XI

**TO BE ABLE TO TELL THE DIFFERENCE
BETWEEN FACT & LIES**

25S – XII

"FEARLESS" REVELATION OF SELF

25S – XIII

TO BECOME UNEMOTIONAL IN ANY CIRCUMSTANCE

25S – XIV

TO CAUSE CHAOS IN ANOTHER'S SORCERY/MAGIC

25S- XV

TO CAUSE ONE TO "DROWN" IN THEIR
OWN LIES

25S – XVI

TO DEPLETE AN ENERGY OR ADVERSARY
OR THE ENERGY OF AN ENEMY

25S – XVII

TO ENCOURAGE DARK ENERGY

25S- XVIII

TO INCREASE ONE'S ABILITY TO DEVELOP RITUAL

25S – XIX

TO KNOW WHAT LURKS BEHIND & TO MANAGE IT

25S – XX

TO NOT LOSE YOUR PATH IN THE PRESENCE OF OTHER INFLUENCES - TO NOT BE A CHAMELEON

25S – XXI

TO OPEN UP VOIDS

25S – XXII

TO PROJECT YOUR NON-TOOL CEREBRAL
SORCERY

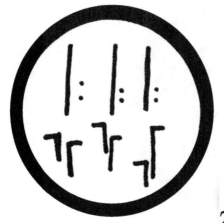

25S – XXIII

**TO RISE ABOVE PETTINESS EVEN IF IT IS
YOUR NATURE TO SUCCUMB**

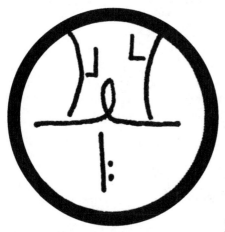

25S - XXIV

**KNOW THE DIFFERENCE BETWEEN FACTS
& LIES**

25S – XXV

LISTEN - TO TRUST YOUR INSTINCTS

<u>NOTES</u>

<u>I</u> - TO RELEASE YOURSELF FROM THE TRAPS OF KINDNESS, SOCIAL MORES, AND FOREGIVENESS

<u>II</u> - TO REMAIN FOCUSED

<u>III</u> - TO RE-SET

<u>IV</u> - TO SEPARATE ONE FROM POTENTIAL PROPERTY

<u>V</u> - TO UNCOVER TRUTH

<u>VI</u> - TO UNDERSTAND SORCERY

<u>VII</u> - UNLOCK FURTHER RESEARCH WHICH MAY BE RESTRICTED

<u>VIII</u> - TO USE SEX IN A PERSUASIVE WAY

IX - ENACT VENGANCE ANNONYMOUSLY

X - WEIGHT LOSS

XI - TO BE ABLE TO DISTINGUISH BETWEEN FACTS & LIES

XII - "FEARLESS" REVELATION OF THE SELF

XIII - TO BECOME UNEMOTIONAL IN ANY CIRCUMSTANCE

XIV - TO CAUSE CHAOS IN ANOTHER'S SORCERY/MAGIC

XV - TO CAUSE ONE TO DROWN IN THEIR OWN LIES

XVI TO DEPLETE AN ENERGY, AN ADVERSARY OR THE ENERGY OF AN ENEMY

XVII - TO ENCOURAGE DARK ENERGY

XVIII - TO INCREASE ONE'S ABILITY TO DEVELOP RITUAL

XIX - TO KNOW WHAT LURKS BEHIND & TO MANAGE IT

XX - TO NOT LOSE YOUR PATH IN THE PRESENCE OF OTHER INFLUENCES - TO NOT BE A CHAMELEON

XXI -TO OPEN UP VOIDS

XXII -TO PROJECT YOUR NON-TOOL CEREBRAL SORCERY

XXIII - TO RISE ABOVE PETTINESS EVEN IF IT IS YOUR NATURE TO SUCCUMB

XXIV - KNOW THE DIFFERENCE BETWEEN FACTS & LIES

XXV – LISTEN -TO TRUST YOUR INSTINCTS

SECTION III - UTILIZATION

I – TO RELEASE YOURSELF FROM THE TRAPS OF KINDNESS, SOCIAL MORES, AND FOREGIVENESS

OVERVIEW

This is a caustic Sigil, by which I mean that the visuals are meant to cause a discomfort – a rift between the comfort zone and/or socially acceptable behavior. The sensation of that rift is represented by hard thorns drifting and escaping, their bits moving unpredicably.

DECONSTRUCTION

The sharps and thorns of this interaction move around creating discomfort in a neat package nestled between social norms.

The transition begins with the self **experiencing** the discomfort and getting used to the feeling of not 'fitting into the accepted behavior'. When the Sigil is used on the self it can release the self from these expected behaviors. When used on another, the target becomes harsh and difficult to handle.

In other words using this Sigil on another will cause them to to loose their place in society.

EXECUTION ON THE SELF

Create the Sigil in ink that is best served with an infusion of your Sacred Elixir. Draw the circle first, then the two symmetrical curves, and finally the center piece starting wherever you feel drawn to begin. Use additional Elixir only, no ink, to draw the dots.

ON ANOTHER – as above utilizing their Eixir if possible and if not construct the sigil directly on a photo of their face. In this situation draw the entire sigil in ink without your Elixir. Your Blood should not appear anywhere in this application.

BLOOD APPLICATION

Blood from inside of your lips is best chosen for this procedure.

RITUAL

As soon as it is dry create a Human Compass (choose a center point) and work to the polarity of the South from your centerpoint. This polarity pulls decay into a situation, and in this case you are performing a Sorcery Event which requires that you break free from a habit. Focus on the Sigil and allow it to bring up emotions (students read Triggers for emotions) which will assist you in recalling opportunities lost through the act of apology or conforming. Walk South.

Infuse youself with this process. Once the Sigil has connected with you set it aflame.

SKILLED STUDENTS

Students of my work should consider accessing the Chaos Void when using this sigil. Find a Trigger before entering the work of this sigil. To do so prepares you for a full interaction with the material from the starting point. Do not use the Iron Ring here as seperating yourself is not the desire – rather you are making yourself known in a new environment.

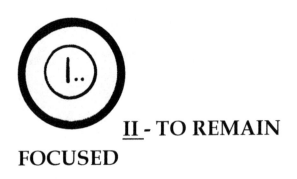

II - TO REMAIN FOCUSED

OVERVIEW

New data suggests that the average person "checks" their phone one hundred and ten times in any given twenty four hour period. Granted much of that is within the process of their work – however for many it is simply the way they function and communicate.

I offer this data as a baseline from which to discuss this sigil. In most Iron Ring Original Sigils the symbol for the self is the line with two dots.

In this sigil, the symbol is insulated within two circles, the inner one set just a bit above the center of the outer one.

This sigil is best utilized on the self. *By this I am stating that this is a sigil not meant to be used for reflective work as using it on other to increase their ability to concentrate will, at best, focus them on the Practitioner and not on the subject which initially required stronger focus.*

That being said there is an application whereby the practitioner intentionally uses this sigil to create a fascination, from another, toward the Practitioner.

If you choose to use the sigil that way then be advised that you should therefore prepare yourself for a potential stalker, as this is not easily undone. If it is your choice to do so, then you are on a path of potential conflict and confrontation.

DECONSTRUCTION

Use of this Sigil puts the self **inside** of the situation which has been the source of imperfect focus. The inner circle contains the self, and the self's dots are in a position to ground one's thinking and focusing process.

The outer circle, present in nearly all of the Original Iron Ring sigils, in this case reinforces the ability to focus as it becomes a buffer – a moat – disallowing intruders and distractions.

EXECUTION

The suggestion is to paint this sigil in black ink on metal. Parchment is, of course always useful, however in this case metal is more appropriate for the process so if you have metal, use it. As ink does not easily attach to metal it is in the users hands to adjust the process so that the appropriate ink is used.

Metal may be treated with abrasive paper or a large eraser can be rubbed on the area prior to utilizing the ink. These methods in combination with the correct and best ink for the metal of choice will yield a desired outcome.

This sigil is drawn by creating the outer circle, then the inner one, followed by the line from top to bottom, and finally the two dots starting with the one on the right and moving toward the line by the completion of the dot closer to the line.

BLOOD APPLICATION

Harvest your Blood from anywhere above your heart by pinprick, taking care not to work near any major Blood vessels. You will need a tiny drop as you will only be anointing the two dots in the same order in which they were drawn.

RITUAL

Place the finished sigil above your head so that you must look up to see it. It should be on a wall or hung in a way that it is perfectly vertical and flush with the wall. Stand in front of the sigil and bring to mind something about which you have considerable knowledge.

While making eye contact with the sigil attempt to confuse yourself or forget the knowledge you have about the chosen subject and then make full eye contact with the sigil while allowing the confusion to dissipate. The activity of honing this sigil to a system of knowledge of which you already have mastery 'teaches' it to bring you into focus and concentration while addressing the issue or subject during which you have not had strong focus. Do this exercise daily until you experience the TRIGGER effect of the sigil on your ability to focus. Keep the sigil in place for as long as you need it. This particular sigil can continue to be used in this matter indefinitely as it becomes talismanic so only one is necessary.

SKILLED STUDENTS
Students of my work should consider entering the Static Practice prior to working this sigil every time.

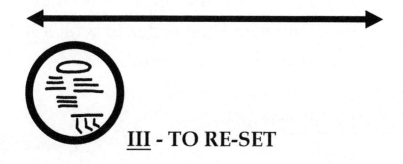

III - TO RE-SET

OVERVIEW
This sigil is built to bring the user back from a moment or period of chaos or stress.

DECONSTRUCTION

The sigil is constructed from the image I have seen when working with Daemons. This is a unique reoccurring image and it has been presented often when a Daemon has been cleared from a space (not from a person). When it appears it enters in sections and the order in which it evolves is rarely repeated.

EXECUTION

Draw this sigil on thick paper or parchment starting with the oval and then go forward adding the lines in a manner in which you are comfortable. It is best constructed when drawn from coal or graphite. When all pieces are drawn complete the outer circle.

BLOOD APPLICATION

This sigil benefits from a smearing of your Blood across all of its components. Harvest by short incision from below your knees. Rub your fingers into the Blood and immediately smear it on the sigil. Use enough to be seen clearly on the sigil.

The **ACT OF** smearing the Blood IS the re-set strength of this sigil. A sensation of being pushed through your own reflection will occur, followed by a minor fog and a sense of chaos surrounding information. By this I mean that one may or may not have a sensation that they possess knowledge or sense of place followed by vacillation of certainty.

RITUAL

Once the Practitioner has experienced the exchanges mentioned above, then it is time to revisit the sigil itself and let it dissipate.

Place another drop of Blood on the back of the sigil – on the blank side of the paper. **Inhale** the spot of Blood and burn the sigil setting it aflame outdoors in the most elaborate manner you can. Make sure all bits of the paper have burned. Pay no attention to the ashes – simply walk away.

SKILLED STUDENTS

Students of my work should consider putting the image of the burning sigil in The Boxes and moving it quickly forward into the future for continued effect.

IV - TO SEPARATE ONE FROM POTENTIAL PROPERTY

OVERVIEW

This sigil is an effigy.

It works by assigning an identity to part of the sigil and forcing a barrier between that identity and its desired property. The word 'property' here is defined by that which the individual seeks to own, be it real estate or intellectual property.

DECONSTRUCTION

Everything above the horizontal center line is the individual upon whom this sigil is directed. The horizontal line represents the work done by the practitioner. The lower third is a symbol used when one desires to redirect energy away from any given individual where LOSS is the desired outcome.

DO NOT use this sigil to dissuade a stalker from their prey. This is a sigil whose function is to separate an individual from ownership of a tangible or intellectual property. Also do not use it to release a property from yourself (example – a house that has been on the market for a long time) unless you are a skilled student.

EXECUTION

Build this sigil from the top down. Draw first the individual, then the horizontal and finish with the lower symbol. Do not draw the surrounding circle until the biological is added (see below).

This sigil is best drawn on wood as it will need to be cut through with energy and malice.

BLOOD APPLICATION
This is an effigy sigil, so therefore your Blood will not be used. A less desirable biological is called for. After the three sections are drawn, THEN use your urine or Menstrual Blood to paint over the horizontal line.

Once this is done then add the outside circle to the sigil.

RITUAL

Once the sigil is prepared as above then prepare a ground space with Grave Soil (to represent the Death of the connection) meeting up at a straight line to dried lifeless leaves.

Your own attachment to herbs or botanicals should be considered here. A "Death aspect" is required in the dried foliage. Do NOT use flowers. The foliage side of this set up must be facing SOUTH from your stance.

Place the grave dirt and the dried botanicals next to each other, just touching up against each other. Place the sigil so that the horizontal line sits on the demarcation between the soil and the botanical with the effigy side resting in the botanical. At this moment add additional urine to the horizontal line and while it is still damp saw through the wood. Leave it there to be taken by the elements. The individual will not secure the property.

SKILLED STUDENTS

Students of my work can add an external Iron Ring to the section placed in the Grave Dirt to further solidify a blockage of opportunity for the individual going forward.

Work this sigil by painting it on your inner wrist with the head of the individual in your palm of your hand. Using the techniques we have discussed concerning the art of Tonic Immobility.

To release a property from the self, do all the work as listed and move the work in The Boxes to prior to purchase or attainment. This will facilitate a sale.

←——————————————→

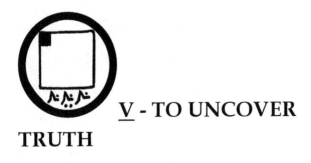

<u>V</u> - TO UNCOVER TRUTH

OVERVIEW

This sigil is meant to uncover truth that is either intentionally hidden or hidden through time, distance, or circumstance.

DECONSTRUCTION

The big box is the truth you seek. The small inner one is your desire to uncover this truth. The symbols beneath represent obstacles – human, circumstantial or Daemonic.

EXECUTION

Build this sigil from sand sprinkled from your hand starting from the small box and working the lower symbols left to right. Finish with the lower two dots.

BLOOD APPLICATION

Harvest your Blood from the palm of your right hand.

RITUAL

Once the sigil is created place a marker (photo, document etc.) representing that information about which you seek truth into the large box and touching the small inner box.

Brush away all of the symbols beneath the box apart from the two lower dots. Add a dot of Blood to the two dots thereby creating a third dot. Leave the work to be absorbed by natural elements.

SKILLED STUDENTS

Stand in the Static Practice. Produce only the materials that represent the question at hand. Observe the sigil in its entirety. Utilize the chaos void and pull REQUIREMENT for truth across onto the materials. Puncture and Bleed into the Chaos Void.

⬅━━━━━━━━━━━━━━━━━━━━━➡

<u>VI</u> - TO UNDERSTAND SORCERY

OVERVIEW

This sigil is not as simple as it appears. It is one of the few in this book that utilizes Dark space in this particular manner. There will be others in the next one of this series. The universe is seventy percent Dark Matter. To do Sorcery one must learn to utilize this matter.

DECONSTRUCTION

The self is deconstructed in this sigil. Iron Ring sigils usually present the self as a vertical line with two or more dots. In this sigil the self is considered embedded in the Darkened circle, as if many versions of the self are standing alongside of themselves joining in with the energy of Sorcery to create this thickened place. The two white dots are the **reflection of the self** in the Dark Matter.

The white area around the Dark sphere is the baggage we abandon – that sense of what has been drilled into us – the information that Sorcery cannot be real. This is a void. All voids fill themselves. The desire in order to perform Sorcery is to remain in the Dark Matter which allows us to manipulate energy in order to utilize the void.

EXECUTION
Draw this sigil just as it is with black ink containing your Blood. Use thick pure white paper made of cotton or wood.

BLOOD APPLICATION
Mentioned above in EXECUTION

RITUAL

Draw this sigil and focus on it until you fall asleep. Take note of your dreams and they will provide additional information to your study and practice.

SKILLED STUDENTS

Create this sigil entirly in the Elixir harvested from one single location along the center meridian of the body. Use the Sleep Sigils (from Flatline) to enhance sleep experiences and use as above to broaden your gaze during sleep. Read between the lines here....

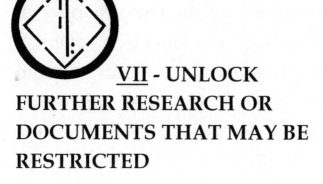

<u>VII</u> - UNLOCK FURTHER RESEARCH OR DOCUMENTS THAT MAY BE RESTRICTED

OVERVIEW

This sigil is useful when one has a perception that there is material available to which one is not privy, and one has a desire to attain said materials.

DECONSTRUCTION

The sigil quite directly places one inside the desired material with additional strengths of acuity of perception with strengthened or even eidetic memory.

EXECUTION

Draw this sigil on some manner of appreciated document – even a newspaper would qualify should one not have any other documents of merit. Be very specific about the straight lines. Do not freehand these lines. They should be carefully executed with a precise straight edge.

BLOOD APPLICATION

Pulse point harvests are best for this work although they require caution so that the user does not puncture a Blood vessel. Anoint the dots and the two small vertical lines with your Blood.

RITUAL

Place the sigil in an envelope and mail it to yourself. Multiple hands will come in contact with the envelope and this redistribution of energy is important. Upon its arrival a trigger will be enacted within the Practitioner and that trigger will inspire strategy and Sorcery to all for the access to the materials which are desired.

SKILLED STUDENTS

Once the sigil is mailed, work in the Chaos void pulling materials from the Chaos side into your project which will be on the void side. If this is done precisely one may have the materials before the envelope arrives.

VIII - TO USE SEX IN A PERSUASIVE WAY

OVERVIEW

Requires no explanation.

DECONSTRUCTION

The self and the secret self exist between two lines which are desirous of intertwining.

EXECUTION

Draw the outer circle in Black ink which contains Iron.

An iron nail in your ink for more than a week will infuse the ink with the energy of the iron desired for this process. Draw the center vertical line and all three dots in your Blood. Best that this be arterial Blood. It is not a simple procedure to procure Blood of this type so if you are not able to do so then use Blood harvested from the pubic mound. This harvest requires a small puncture NOT an incision.

The two curvaceous lines are best drawn as follows:

One in ink containing semen

One in ink containing menstrual Blood.

It is completely irrelevant if you are a man or woman, and if you are intending to use this sigil (which becomes a talisman) to persuade a man or woman. This is the requirement for this sigil. If these materials are difficult for you to come by consider that Sorcerers should have individuals in their circle who will give them these materials.

BLOOD APPLICATION
See above.

RITUAL

Keep this sigil in contact with your skin during masturbation. During masturbation visualize the endeavor you are constructing. This is now a talisman and the work will proceed as desired.

SKILLED STUDENTS

This can be used during a sexual encounter and the third dot can be the Blood/Sexual fluids of the other. You have been taught the cautions and techniques of this procedure.

IX - ENACT VENGANCE ANNONYMOUSLY

OVERVIEW

This interesting thing about anonymous vengeance is that part of the amusement is watching the target try to decode its origin... If the target is one who is not frequently in the company of Sorcerers then you will stand out rather quickly.

DECONSTRUCTION

This too is an exclusive combination, derivative from Nordic roots.

EXECUTION

Create this sigil with sticks or dowels for the straight lines inside the circle where you have drawn all of the other parts in black ink. The inked portions are the 'game board' if you will.

BLOOD APPLICATION

One simple dot of your Blood is required in the small circle to anoint the board.

RITUAL

Once the board is ready, place an image of the target inside the large circle and begin to place the sticks in one at a time, taking one's own cue to the pacing.

Some do this in the course of a night – some in a year, this is a personal choice. Each piece further entraps the target in this act of vengeance. The vengeance is derived from the target's own weaknesses.

SKILLED STUDENTS
Utilize an envocation of Chagatathy for a perfect icing on this cake....

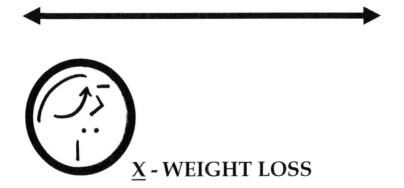

X - WEIGHT LOSS

OVERVIEW

This sigil is based on the idea that if you want something you have never had you must do something you have never done.

DECONSTRUCTION

The self is deconstructed in this sigil. The energy of the self floats above it, and the rest is a useful visualization of picking and choosing when utilizing The Chaos Void (one of the 4 Pillars of my work). Many readers will not be familiar with The Chaos Void so I will present this ritual here in a simplified use (skilled students see below).

EXECUTION

Build this sigil by drawing it in chalk on a surface that receives chalk well. Create it in large format – over a foot in diameter. It must be on a wall or on something that can be hung on a wall. Draw the self first, then the remaining symbols. Finish with the circle. When done, add the Blood application.

BLOOD APPLICATION

Harvest your Blood from an area/s of your body that represent the most discomfort in the area of weight. Paint the dots with that Blood.

RITUAL

Place your hand on either side of the sigil and work your hands towards it as if your hands are magnetized to the wall causing slow deliberate movements.   As your hands approach the outer circle allow them to smudge the circle until it begins to lose its structure. Work this way until the entire circle is smudged NEVER lifting your hands from the wall.   Distractions WILL occur during this process.   Your phone will ring – you will get an itch and this sort of thing.   IGNORE these distractions.

Once the circle is smudged, lift your hands and allow your fingers to explore the symbols above the Self, (remember the self is a straight line with two dots), lightly touching the symbols to hone to them. After a considerable exploration touch each symbol and drag a smudge of it to either side of the Self, representing its new location. The symbols will not move, however the smudge will be a representation of the move.

SKILLED STUDENTS

Produce this sigil with chalk in the "air" inside of the iron ring. Walk through the sigil. That is all that is necessary to place the energy of the sigil inside of the self.

XI - TO BE ABLE TO TELL THE DIFFERENCE BETWEEN FACT & LIES

OVERVIEW

This sigil is a divination sigil. It allows the Practitioner to have an experience of heightened intuitive knowing.

DECONSTRUCTION

All pieces of this sigil are a private development of this author and should be seen as one complete image.

EXECUTION

Because it is one complete image the sequence of drawing is irrelevant with one exception. **The outer circle is drawn last.** Draw this sigil completely in your Blood on thick paper made from wood or cotton.

BLOOD APPLICATION

Harvest your Blood from areas of your body that have the least amount of hair follicles. Collect it in a vial and use it to paint this sigil.

RITUAL

Make a brush out of your own hair if it has not been color treated or the hair of a child or infant. **Do not obtain the hair without permission.**

Paint the sigil at night utilizing the darkness for the clarity it provides. When it is completely dry rest the sigil on a pile of iron nails. Holding strong magnets in your hands, hover your hands above the sigil. The work here will render the intuitive process of your Blood into an energy that is connected to magnetic principles. From this point your intuitive knowing will increase. Work this exercise often and do experiments, collect data and note the increase in your ability to know the truth from lies.

SKILLED STUDENTS

Enter the Static Practice. Stay in it long enough to feel the sense of separation between yourself and the supporting structure (where you are sitting). When that sense of elevation/separation exists then do the above ritual. Whatever you attain within the state of being in the Static Practice will be a permanent layer of skill. Work here in this way until you can no longer focus. By doing this you are imbedding the skill layer. The loss of focus is the proof of the plug in.

⟵———————————————⟶

<u>XII</u> - "FEARLESS"
REVELATION OF THE SELF

OVERVIEW

This sigil is built to create a clear view of the self from the perspective of the Practitioner. It is NOT a third party sigil.

DECONSTRUCTION

The sigil is built to present the hidden from the known aspects of the self. The upper right corner presents a darkened place. That is the known. All else is unknown.

Tangents from that darkened place are the comfort zone of the "perhaps known". Two interlocking symbols further away present the unknown self. The distance between the two sections present the work to be done. In this sigil the outer circle is particularly relevant.

EXECUTION

Create the outer ring on paper which is relevant to the Practitioner. It is a personal choice. For some it could be parchment, for others newspaper...there is no right answer, only a personal one.

Over three days which follow nights containing dreams which are remembered by the Practitioner, anoint the circle with freshly harvested Blood.

There may be days **between** these harvest days as the work days must follow nights filled with dreams which are clearly remembered by the practitioner. The amount of days which pass is as personal as the paper on which the sigil is drawn.

After the third day of fortifying the circle with your Blood, another night of recalled dreams must pass. After that night draw the upper right group of symbols and fill the dark area in with your Blood.

Again, another night of recalled dreams must pass, then draw the interlocking symbols WITH YOUR BLOOD.

Set the entire sigil aside. On the next day following recalled dreams, the Practitioner must place the sigil under clothing with the drawn side pressing against the sternum and leave it there for 24 hours.

Remove the sigil and set it aside until another night of recalled dreams.

Note the content of these dreams.

If they are unusual or disturbing, burn the sigil and smear the ashes on pulse points. Let the ashes fade naturally. If the dreams or not unusual or disturbing then wait for a night during which unusual or disturbing dreams present themselves, and proceed thusly with the burning of the sigil.

BLOOD APPLICATION

For this sigil execution, Blood application and Ritual are all one as described above.

RITUAL

For this sigil execution, Blood application and Ritual are all one as described above.

SKILLED STUDENTS

Use dream inticing sigils to create the opportunity to proceed through the work.

XIII - TO BECOME UNEMOTIONAL IN ANY CIRCUMSTANCE

OVERVIEW

This sigil is best used when one is at the mercy of their emotions.

DECONSTRUCTION

This sigil is a root without a tree, disconnected from thought, **without sentiment and powerful in its Death state.**

EXECUTION

Build this sigil from black ink on wood or wood based thick paper. Wood is an absolute requirement for this sigil.

BLOOD APPLICATION

Harvest Blood from the bottom of both feet. Place dabs of it on the thick part of the main symbol.

RITUAL

Utilize this sigil in reflection. By this I mean create it in a state of weak dependency or emotional fragility, creating the sigil in the full throws of the emotion, making the sigil representative of it. Keep the sigil hidden after use. Make a new one each time. Keep them all. Eventually you will have a small stack of them. Bind them together as a talisman to call upon in these moments of weakness and the talisman will assist. Over a short period of time the talisman will "cure" the weakness.

SKILLED STUDENTS

Make the sigil once and freeze it in ice. Leave it there and call upon an image of it while inside the Iron Ring.

←——————————————→

XIV - TO CAUSE CHAOS IN ANOTHER'S SORCERY/MAGIC

OVERVIEW

This sigil is built to scramble another's "signal".

DECONSTRUCTION

The Practitioner is represented by the vertical line on the left, and instead of a dot there is a weapon in the center which projects the intention of the practitioner into the work of another. The work of another is represented by the four interlocking symbols.

EXECUTION

This sigil will work if painted on paper, wood, metal or glass. That being said, it is **best** served by construction which offers raised texture (bas-relief).

Build this sigil from clay, sticks/wood or anything which raised the images and gives them texture. The reverse is also effective, such as wood burning or carving.

Either way create the interlocking images first, then the vertical (Practitioner), followed by the weapon. Finish with the outer circle.

BLOOD APPLICATION

Harvest your Blood from the pad of the index finger on the dominant hand and place it on the weapon.

RITUAL

The creating and anointing of this sigil is part of the ritual. Do it WITH THE INTENDED TARGET in mind. This is **not** a reusable sigil. Create an effigy doll from clay or any medium that if efficient for the practitioner. It does not have to be a magnificent sculpture. A simple stick form will do. It must be small enough to fit on the side of the sigil with the interlocking symbols. Place the effigy on top of that area and face the sigil so that the interlocking sigils are facing South. This is the polarity of decay. Placing that side South automatically by default places the Practitioner side North which is exactly how it is best situated.

Do an additional harvest and use the Blood to spatter across from the Practitioner side onto the effigy. Once the proof is in of the solution, bury the sigil and the effigy together as situated (directionally).

SKILLED STUDENTS
Envoke (my word) GOLOX for greater efficiency in the matter.

 <u>XV</u> - TO CAUSE ONE TO "DROWN" IN THEIR OWN LIES

OVERVIEW

This sigil is built in a manner to cause mental and/or literal drowning. Use with caution.

DECONSTRUCTION

This sigil combines illustrated Blood loss through sharp implement while under water. Think shark bait.....

EXECUTION

Carve this sigil on the flesh of a whole fish. Start with the outer circle, then the curved lines, add the individual's name somewhere attached to a curved line. Then finish with the sharp images cutting in over the name.

BLOOD APPLICATION

Only the biologicals of the target can be used on this sigil. If you do not have any then the name will suffice. If you DO have their biologicals, place the biological on the curved lines as well along with the name. Biologicals have a hierarchy.

Circulatory Blood is best, followed by sexual fluids, breast milk, skin cells, hair follicles, hair, nails, and finally name or effigy. **Do not use menstrual Blood for this sigil as it will backfire on the practitioner.**

RITUAL

Face the image toward the East for speed of delivery. When you feel the connection, immerse the sigil in a clear glass of water (still facing East). Outcomes vary from mental to actual "drowning".

SKILLED STUDENTS

Add magnets behind the glass and iron filings to the water. The outcome will be more extreme.

XVI - TO DEPLETE AN ENERGY OR ADVERSARY OR THE ENERGY OF AN ENEMY

OVERVIEW

CAUTION - This sigil is a dagger. It is not suggested for use as a first rime fore into sigil work. When it "pierces" it causes a **portal through which the adversary's energy falls.**

DECONSTRUCTION

The main staff is a dagger in the shape of the self. The dots are on the opposite side stating defensive stance. The other small curves and lower dash are intentional and must be drawn.

EXECUTION

Draw with black INK (gall ink if possible) on leather starting with the outer circle. Write the name of the target/targets anywhere across the lower half of the circle using black ink. The name must be written in single strokes only. Do not double stroke anywhere on a letter in the name.

Draw the small lower dash first, then the main staff, followed by its embellishments and finally the dots.

BLOOD APPLICATION

Harvest from a location that represents a powerful place to you. Add your Blood to the top curved line and the top dot.

RITUAL

This sigil is best served in full contact. A perfect scenario would be for it to make contact with the skin of the recipient. If that is not possible then somewhere the recipient is known to walk over.

If that is not an option then get a photo/print out of the person or an image representing that person and soak it in milk. Dip the leather in the milk and let it dry before painting the sigil.

Once the sigil is in one of these scenarios place iron and magnets south of the location of the sigil. Work energy to allow for your mind to present a flow of energy "placing: the sigil into the decaying energy of the southern polarity. There is nothing more for you to do now….just watch…

SKILLED STUDENTS

Once the sigil is prepared place a drop of your Blood on a ferrite magnet on the positive side. While using mental acuity to place the sigil South (as written above) – utilize a second aspect of mental imagery to lift the evacuated energy North and into your Blood. When this is done and your Blood is flaked, scrape it off the magnet, add it to a beverage with an alcohol content and rub it into your pulse points. Allow it to dry and fade naturally.

<u>XVII</u> - TO ENCOURAGE DARK ENERGY

OVERVIEW

This sigil is an opportunity to connect with dark matter. As theoretical physicists tell us, the universe is seventy percent dark matter. This is NOT an issue of good/evil.

This is the Science of Sorcery and must be handled as such. If you are either emotionally or morally stuck on these new age fluffy descriptions of dark matter than Sorcery is not for you.

If you desire to move forward and tap the energy of seventy percent of the physical universe, then use this sigil to break free of baggage and move forward.

DECONSTRUCTION
Simple. The balance of utilizing dark and non-dark matter is represented in this sigil. This image in the other circle is the self, willing to take on a new energy.

EXECUTION
Paint this sigil on metal. Use black paint. The circle around the sigil is, in this case, irrelevant. Keep this as a permanent sigil and anoint it as needed (see ritual).

BLOOD APPLICATION

Fingertips. See Execution for need and Ritual for uses and additional directives in this matter.

RITUAL

Use this sigil whenever you are desirous of extending your reach into dark matter. This is a personal choice. Remember that dark matter provides one with seventy percent more energy to use in Sorcery. Harvesting for use on this sigil should always be from fingertips.

Rarely do I suggest that individuals use their fingertips for harvesting as there are more nerve endings there, thereby making the puncture more painful. This sigil is best enacted as a result of a puncture that stimulated large amounts of nerves.

When in need of utilization of this sigil place a drop of Blood on the dark circle and allow yourself a long moment to take in the visual of this experience. This will heighten the energy derived for use in Sorcery.

SKILLED STUDENTS

This is a perfect scenario for the Static Practice. Place yourself into the Static Practice prior to creating the sigil so that it is created in that state of energy.

Set it down and stay in the Static Practice allowing dark energy to ENTER the sigil. This sigil will now be a portal to bring dark energy/matter into your work.

Create a TRIGGER if you have the skill. When you exit the Static Practice this sigil will be memory stamped and you will not need to physically use it unless you find that helpful. If so, anointing it is also optional and may bring excessive energy at a driven pace. Do that ONLY if that is what you are seeking.

MASTER STUDENT
Combine this sigil with
S25XXI - VOIDS for work involving
Striking the Target.

XVIII -TO INCREASE ONE'S ABILITY TO DEVELOP RITUAL

OVERVIEW

This sigil is complex and meant to act as a trigger. Make sure you have the time to have this experience.

DECONSTRUCTION

The self is represented twice, once vertically and once on an upward curve. The remaining symbols will remain a private 'recipe'.

EXECUTION

Draw the sigil on bright white paper and plain black ink. Draw it in any order that feels right. This is an individually enacted experience.

BLOOD APPLICATION

Harvest your Blood from the scalp. Place it on the dots on the top half of the sigil.

RITUAL

When the sigil is constructed place a piece of glass on top of it. Trace over and over on it with your finger until the impression of the sigil is imprinted in your mind. I do not like to use the word 'memorize' as that is not the same as imprinting.

Work this exercise nightly and especially before ritual of any kind. Once the need for the sigil is gone, by which I mean once the image is impressed in your mind, bury the sigil.

SKILLED STUDENTS

Do not physically draw this sigil. Using the image in the book, 'finger draw' the sigil in air and harvest four punctures on your inner arm to represent the dots. Continue to air draw the sigil. The punctures will suffice for the duration of the study.

<u>XIX</u> - TO KNOW WHAT LURKS BEHIND & TO MANAGE IT

OVERVIEW

This sigil is useful as a preemptive strike as well as a defensive mechanism.

DECONSTRUCTION

The self/Practitioner stands solid with weaponry as that which lurks behind a situation - a person's intent, a Daemonic energy or the presence of the Disincarnate - are held at bay by Directional Sorcery.

EXECUTION

Scratch this sigil into metal. That is the best way. Any other method is second best so therefore they are all the same. Work from left to right when creating the sigil. The outer circle is irrelevant.

BLOOD APPLICATION

Harvest your Blood from anywhere on your arms and suck it into your mouth without touching it with your hands. Mix it with saliva and spit it onto the sigil each time you utilize it.

RITUAL

Use chalk or something impermanent to write the name of the situation across the portion of the sigil that looks like ladders. Then spit (See above BLOOD APPLICATION for the most important part of this ritual) so that the spit covers as much of the sigil as possible.

The action of the spitting is just as vital as the Blood itself. Allow the spit to disrupt the chalk, melting away the integrity of the letters. Once the letters are unrecognizable then the sigil has been utilized. Now choose a method of Divination and note the information derived.

There will be external roads from which additional information arrives now as well. Wash the sigil and keep it from the light when it is not in use.

SKILLED STUDENTS

Bite into your lower lip for the Blood source. This is more effective as there is no middle step between the Blood and the spit. When the sigil is all dressed with your biologicals place it in The Boxes and ask it to bring you to a location where the images of that which lurks behind can be seen.

Utilize The Boxes and the EDGE energy of the Iron Ring to see a physical projection of the information. With enough practice you will not need the sigil, just the spatter of Blood and saliva into The Boxes.

XX - TO NOT LOSE YOUR PATH IN THE PRESENCE OF OTHER INFLUENCES - TO NOT BE A CHAMELEON

OVERVIEW

This sigil is best used by those who feel they have a tendency or even a habit of letting go of who they are and taking on the habit, demeanor or even doctrine of others. This habit inhibits the growth and development of the self.

DECONSTRUCTION

The line and dots inside of the circle represent the self, and the self is tending toward dropping down towards the temptation of the influence of others. The inner circle is a preventive measure and the three images on the bottom are constructed from an amalgam of symbols.

These three images represent the most common causes of chameleon-iziation as discovered through data. The desire to be liked or accepted, a simplicity of accommodation to the self or to others for social convention, or a lack of self-development.

EXECUTION

Build this sigil from the inside out on paper or wood starting with the dots, the line, the inner circle, the three lower symbols and then the outer circle.

BLOOD APPLICATION

Harvest your Blood from a comfortable place and anoint the dots with it. Arterial/assessable Blood is utilized in this Sigil work.

RITUAL

Utilize this prepared sigil by carrying it with you and noting when you are acting in a chameleon-like manner. After each of three of these acknowledged experiences re-anoint the sigil placing the Elixir on the line. After all three times burn the sigil to ash outdoors and leave the ash where it sits to be taken away by natural occurrence (wind, rain, etc.)

SKILLED STUDENTS

Draw this on a mirror in your Blood. Let it dry and flake. Carry the flaked Blood in a vile for a period of time until it becomes burdensome to do. Then add gall ink to the vial, draw the sigil again and burn it as above.

XXI -TO OPEN UP VOIDS

OVERVIEW

This sigil is meant to create voids and widen existing voids. Voids are a tool we, in the Science of Sorcery utilize often. Remember, especially those of you who have an understanding of physics, that all voids become filled....the question we ask in the Science of Sorcery is- with what do we desire to fill these voids?

DECONSTRUCTION

The square contains two crossed lines which are, for the purpose of this deconstruction not two crossed lines, rather 4 intersecting lines. The two verticals represent the self in the way that we know ourselves to be, our habits, tastes, etc...

The two horizontal lines represent that which flows within us which we cannot simply define. The entire structure is supported by a box with hard right angles so that the structure is protected.

The other symbols are voids. They are present outside of the box and accessible. The Box can either be protection from the voids or a lure to bring them closer. The use depends wholly upon the desire of the Practitioner.

EXECUTION
Paint this sigil on clear glass. Use a permanent paint.

Paint both sides so that the sigil has texture on both sides of the glass. Create this sigil in a fashion so that it lasts. This sigil has an essence of talismanic energy.

BLOOD APPLICATION
Harvest your Blood from an area of your body that has the least hair follicles. Place a drop of your Blood into a small glass vial. Set it aside.

RITUAL
Stand the glass so that it is held up by two large magnets drawing toward one another. The magnets form the stand.

To bring voids (empty spaces for opportunity) in – face the sigil standing North (utilizing the polarity of increase) and place the vial behind it. This will bring voids (opportunity) into your DNA. Remember that all voids will fill so be conservative about the excessive opening of voids. To shut down voids, reverse the entire set up toward the South. This polarity pulls away from the Blood clearing away unwanted voids. This is NOT the same as filling the voids.

SKILLED STUDENTS

Place iron filings or small nails fully made of iron into the vial.

This will hasten the outcome of the work. **DO NOT DO THIS** if you are not well studied in the Pillar of Directional Sorcery.

XXII -TO PROJECT YOUR NON-TOOL CEREBRAL SORCERY

OVERVIEW

This sigil is the self-projected upon another situation or person.

It is, in this form, a sigil. However it is actually a weapon. Read on…

DECONSTRUCTION

The image represents the self projecting itself upon something else. It has a symbol for its backstory, intention, a containment for its power and a varied group of targets.

EXECUTION

Paint it on Iron or Steel starting with the center split vertical line, then the lines on the left, the small squares and finally the horizontal lines and the small circle. The outer circle is last.

BLOOD APPLICATION

Harvest your Blood from five locations and place it on all of the lines.

RITUAL

There is very little instruction for this sigil for those not skilled in my Four Pillars of Sorcery. For those of you who are not skilled, the construction itself will begin to open the portal to the abilities of non-tool Sorcery. Once it is constructed keep it and be mindful of its capacity to build triggers.

SKILLED STUDENTS

Utilize the language of influence by communicating your desire for increased ability in this area by **communicating** with your Blood.

Impress in scratches or pressure the image of this sigil on your flesh and utilize the Iron Ring for projection. After the first usage place it in a permanent spot in the Iron Ring so that it is available without hesitation. For the advanced student there is no benefit in the paper drawing of this sigil – and extraordinary benefit from the method of scratch or pressure and use of the Iron Ring.

MASTER STUDENT
"CLIP" this sigil. Know it.

←——————————————————→

XXIII - TO RISE ABOVE PETTINESS EVEN IF IT IS YOUR NATURE TO SUCCUMB

OVERVIEW

This sigil is best applied when one finds themselves wrought with time consumed by the minutia of analyzing the nature of other and their intentions. This Sigil is built to cause one to observe their own involvement in the need to succumb to the pettiness of others.

DECONSTRUCTION

The sigil offers three versions of the self. They rise above gritty angular interruptions which may rise and fall and cause disruption or open and close and swallow the self by eating away at valuable time.

EXECUTION

As the wasting of time is deadly, then the materials in which this sigil is created must reflect the complete lack of the value of pettiness.

Create this Sigil on the thinnest paper you can find, tissue paper or otherwise.

Create this sigil so that it is no bigger than an inch or so in diameter. Create it in black ink starting with the three vertical lines and their accompanying dots as they represent you. Then add the lower symbols, finally add the ring.

BLOOD APPLICATION

Blood should be added to the three images that represent the self. Paint over them with your harvested Elixir. I find it is best to use Blood Harvested from your mouth for this sigil.

RITUAL

When the sigil is finished and dry, bake this sigil in an oven or put it in strong sunlight. It must be "cremated" by a slow desiccation. Any remaining pieces should be smeared on ones feet to presume consumption of the behavioral repair.

SKILLED STUDENTS

Skilled students should create the sigil in the same manner. Then when it is ready use South facing Directional Sorcery to deteriorate the connection between the self and the unwanted behavior.

During South facing Directional Sorcery place the sigil into a glass and pour red wine or another spirit over it. Allow it to sit in the glass during the South facing Directional Sorcery.

When you are satisfied with your work, pour the liquid into another glass and drink it without the sigil in the new glass. When you are done dry out the sigil and burn it, leaving the ashes to be taken by wind.

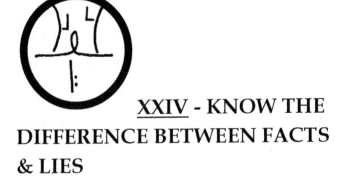

<u>XXIV</u> - KNOW THE DIFFERENCE BETWEEN FACTS & LIES

OVERVIEW

This sigil is meant to be used in critical situations where knowing what is true and what is not will significantly change the outcome of the situation.

DECONSTRUCTION

All sigils are unique. This one is particularly interesting as the energy of working with the sigil is displayed within the sigil itself.

A loop sits between two slightly different versions of a symbol. They are similar in so much as they truth and lies are often similar or portrayed to be so as to create confusion.

The loop is the action of utilizing this sigil to distinguish between truths and lies. The self sits below the interaction so that the work is cerebral, delivering the outcome to the visceral self.

EXECUTION
Build this sigil from clay or another medium that can be broken (not torn). Even a cracker or crisp of some kind is useful in this execution.

The image is to be drawn in the following manner. Create the outside ring first, then draw the images from the bottom up, i.e., first the self (vertical line), then the dots, followed by the loop, and finally the two images representing truth and lies.

BLOOD APPLICATION

Blood is not needed for work with this sigil.

RITUAL

When the sigil is complete expose it to images of or items pertaining to the subject at hand.

For example if one is making an effort to determine the truthfulness of a spouse, an image of that individual or a marriage certificate will do.

Place the cracker face down on the image and leave it there while you do something unrelated to this work. Return to the sigil and place the cracker face down on the image. Puncture the palm of your hand with a pin so that a drop of blood escapes, (either palm will do). Turn the cracker clockwise many times making no notice of where the image is or how it is focused.

Press your palm down upon the cracker and crush it in place. Set two magnets, one alongside the work on either side.

Step away from the work for a time and do another activity. When you return bits of the cracker will have moved right or left toward the magnets. The magnet on the left represents the truth. If that is where the cracker bits have gone, then the energy of the crushing has produced enough of a force of energy to have the individual at hand reveal their truths and lies either through their own admission or through residual exposure.

If the crumbs have moved to the right, then repeat the work with greater force and intent.

SKILLED STUDENTS
Create as suggested. However create a non physical effigy of yourself inside of the Iron Ring and "feed" the cracker to it…..

XXV – LISTEN -TO TRUST YOUR INSTINCTS

OVERVIEW

This sigil is an instrument of insight into self-trust, specifically instinct. What we hear in our minds "voice" is often dismissed and one chooses to follow an external voice instead. This, more often than not, does not result in the best possible outcome.

DECONSTRUCTION

The symbols in this sigil are an amalgam of the ear bones, the strings of a harp and several alchemical symbols. Each of these original inspirations address the "hearing" of one's voice. **There is additional content in these illustrations which I will keep in reserve for my students.**

EXECUTION

This is a sigil that benefits from inclusion into flesh. Build this sigil by carving it into your flesh and using the Bleeding incisions as a stamper. Dab parchment onto the incisions and create a perfect Blood image of the sigil.

BLOOD APPLICATION

As the full directive for this sigil involves Blood, the EXECUTION listed above gives the start point.

Cut or scratch this into a hairless place on your body.

RITUAL

When the sigil is complete and the parchment is dry place the parchment version on a large ceramic ferrite magnet. Chip off a piece of the magnet and carry it with you. Tend as little as possible to the incisions apart from keeping them clean enough to avoid infection. Touch the magnet to the incision. This will hone the magnet as well. The desire is to hone oneself to trust one's own Blood – one's own instinct. The Parchment version should rest on the magnets for several days and nights until the incisions have healed. When it is so, place the parchment sigil in a frame with glass. Display so that you can see the sigil daily.

SKILLED STUDENTS

The area of the incisions should be "lifted" into The Boxes and dragged back and forth through your time line. The parchment sigil is best placed on the quiet side of the Chaos Void. Do this work in the Static Practice.

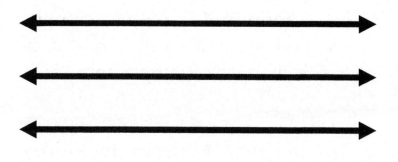

RITUALS – SENTENCES AND STORIES USING MULTIPLE SIGILS

The following is an example of how to combine sigils into a broader event. Combining sigils is a method of constructing a Sorcery sentence or story. These are useful when the desire is to restructure or deconstruct a situation that is complex. Complex situations must be addressed with complex solutions as sigil work is best done in this manner of comparison.

RITUAL

To deconstruct blocks to Sorcery and reset, refine and hone your energy to address the work. For SKILLED STUDENTS this can be utilized as 4 Pillars Honing.

When constructing a long sigil statement it is best to choose sigils with similar requirements for construction. If that is not possible make adjustments where possible to create similarities in construction.

In this ritual all of these sigils are to be drawn on paper. Choose a paper that suits you. This is Sorcery – the Practitioner – and ONLY the Practitioner needs to be satisfied...

Here are the Sigils you will need. Read the Directives below before beginning.

25S -VIII – TO RESET
25S -VII – TO FOCUS
25S -XII – "Fearless" revelation of the SELF
25S -XIII – To become Unemotional in any circumstance

25S -XVI - To Deplete an Energy or Adversary or the energy of an enemy
25S -XVIII - To Increase One's Ability to Develop Ritual

These 6 Sigils form a ritual. The amount of time taken between Sigils is personal as part of the development is to learn to listen to your own pacing – your own experience. Take notes, keep data....this is vital to your continued development in the Science of Sorcery. Proceed....

SORCERESS CAGLIASTRO
Blood Sorceress, Necromancer in the hands of 9

CONTACT, STUDY or FOR CONSULTATIONS, READINGS or NECROMANCY SESSIONS
www.cagliastrotheironring.com
or email your enquiry to
sorceresscagliastro@gmail.com

To study these materials as a core student in weekly classes visit

www.cagliastrotheironring.com
Click on the Wednesday Night Core Classes page and obtain a 4 week package. The classes are on-going.

SORCERESS CAGLIASTRO
Blood Sorceress, Necromancer in the hands of 9

an IRON RING PRODUCT

Printed in Great Britain
by Amazon